50 International Breakfast Food Recipes

By: Kelly Johnson

Table of Contents

- Shakshuka (Middle Eastern)
- Croissants (French)
- Chilaquiles (Mexican)
- Eggs Benedict (American)
- Full English Breakfast (British)
- Biryani (Indian)
- Pancakes (American)
- Açaí Bowl (Brazilian)
- Smoothie Bowl (Global)
- Nasi Lemak (Malaysian)
- Samosas (Indian)
- Frittata (Italian)
- Huevos Rancheros (Mexican)
- Bircher Müesli (Swiss)
- French Toast (American)
- Porridge (British)
- Dim Sum (Chinese)
- Arepas (Venezuelan)
- Bagels with Cream Cheese (Jewish)
- Misal Pav (Indian)
- Gallo Pinto (Costa Rican)
- Breakfast Tacos (American)
- Ramen (Japanese)
- Uji (Tanzanian)
- Poff Poff (Nigerian)
- Scones (British)
- Tosti (Dutch)
- Kanom Krok (Thai)
- Ceviche de Corvina (Peruvian)
- Sausage Rolls (British)
- Dosa (Indian)
- Tzatziki with Pita (Greek)
- Tamagoyaki (Japanese)
- Lox and Bagel (Jewish)
- Shakshuka (North African)

- Aloo Paratha (Indian)
- Pão de Queijo (Brazilian)
- Faworki (Polish)
- Tteokbokki (Korean)
- Koshari (Egyptian)
- Poached Eggs with Spinach (Global)
- Plov (Uzbek)
- Quiche (French)
- Kachori (Indian)
- Tortilla Española (Spanish)
- Matzah Brei (Jewish)
- Puto (Filipino)
- Brekfast Burrito (American)
- Idli (Indian)
- Tostadas (Mexican)

Shakshuka (Middle Eastern)

Ingredients:

- 2 tbsp olive oil
- 1 onion, diced
- 1 bell pepper, diced
- 4 cloves garlic, minced
- 1 can (28 oz) diced tomatoes
- 1 tsp ground cumin
- 1 tsp paprika
- Salt and pepper to taste
- 6 large eggs
- Fresh parsley for garnish

Instructions:

Heat olive oil in a large skillet over medium heat. Sauté onion and bell pepper until softened. Add garlic, cumin, and paprika, cooking for another minute. Pour in diced tomatoes and season with salt and pepper. Simmer for 10-15 minutes until thickened. Create small wells in the sauce and crack eggs into each well. Cover and cook until the eggs are set. Garnish with fresh parsley before serving.

Croissants (French)

Ingredients:

- 4 cups all-purpose flour
- 1/4 cup sugar
- 1 tbsp salt
- 2 1/4 tsp active dry yeast
- 1 1/4 cups milk, warmed
- 1 cup unsalted butter, cold
- 1 egg, for egg wash

Instructions:

In a bowl, combine flour, sugar, salt, and yeast. Stir in warm milk and mix until a dough forms. Knead for 5 minutes, then let it rise for 1 hour. Roll the dough into a rectangle and place cold butter in the center. Fold the dough over the butter and roll it out. Repeat the folding and rolling process three times. Cut the dough into triangles, roll them into croissants, and place on a baking sheet. Let rise for 30 minutes. Preheat the oven to 400°F (200°C) and brush croissants with egg wash. Bake for 15-20 minutes until golden brown.

Chilaquiles (Mexican)

Ingredients:

- 8 corn tortillas, cut into triangles
- 1 cup salsa (red or green)
- 4 large eggs
- 1/2 cup queso fresco, crumbled
- 1/4 cup sour cream
- Fresh cilantro for garnish

Instructions:

In a skillet, fry tortilla triangles until crispy and golden. Remove and set aside. In the same skillet, add salsa and bring to a simmer. Stir in the fried tortillas, ensuring they are coated. In another pan, fry eggs sunny-side up. Serve chilaquiles topped with fried eggs, crumbled queso fresco, sour cream, and fresh cilantro.

Eggs Benedict (American)

Ingredients:

- 2 English muffins, split
- 4 large eggs
- 4 slices Canadian bacon
- 1/2 cup hollandaise sauce
- Fresh chives for garnish

Instructions:

Poach eggs in simmering water for about 3-4 minutes until whites are set. Meanwhile, toast English muffin halves and sauté Canadian bacon until warmed. Assemble by placing a slice of bacon on each muffin half, topping with a poached egg and drizzling with hollandaise sauce. Garnish with chopped chives before serving.

Full English Breakfast (British)

Ingredients:

- 2 sausages
- 2 slices bacon
- 2 eggs
- 1 tomato, halved
- 1 cup baked beans
- 2 slices black pudding (optional)
- 2 slices toast
- Butter for toast

Instructions:

In a large skillet, cook sausages and bacon until browned. Remove and set aside. In the same skillet, fry eggs to your liking and add tomato halves to cook until softened. Heat baked beans in a small pot. If using, fry black pudding slices until crispy. Serve everything on a plate with buttered toast.

Biryani (Indian)

Ingredients:

- 2 cups basmati rice
- 1 lb chicken or vegetables
- 1 onion, thinly sliced
- 2 tomatoes, chopped
- 4 cloves garlic, minced
- 1 tbsp ginger, minced
- 2 tsp biryani spice mix
- 1/4 cup yogurt
- Fresh cilantro and mint for garnish

Instructions:

Rinse rice and soak for 30 minutes. In a large pot, heat oil and sauté onions until golden. Add garlic, ginger, and biryani spice mix, cooking for another minute. Stir in chicken or vegetables and cook until browned. Add tomatoes, yogurt, and rice, mixing well. Pour in 4 cups of water, bring to a boil, then reduce heat, cover, and simmer until rice is cooked, about 20 minutes. Garnish with fresh cilantro and mint before serving.

Pancakes (American)

Ingredients:

- 1 cup all-purpose flour
- 2 tbsp sugar
- 1 tsp baking powder
- 1/2 tsp baking soda
- 1/4 tsp salt
- 1 cup buttermilk
- 1 large egg
- 2 tbsp melted butter
- Maple syrup for serving

Instructions:

In a bowl, whisk together flour, sugar, baking powder, baking soda, and salt. In another bowl, mix buttermilk, egg, and melted butter. Combine wet and dry ingredients until just mixed. Heat a skillet over medium heat and pour in batter to form pancakes. Cook until bubbles form, then flip and cook until golden brown. Serve warm with maple syrup.

Açaí Bowl (Brazilian)

Ingredients:

- 2 packets frozen açaí puree
- 1 banana, sliced
- 1/2 cup almond milk
- 1/4 cup granola
- Fresh fruits for topping (berries, banana, etc.)
- Honey for drizzling (optional)

Instructions:

In a blender, combine frozen açaí puree, banana, and almond milk. Blend until smooth. Pour into a bowl and top with granola, fresh fruits, and a drizzle of honey if desired. Serve immediately.

Smoothie Bowl (Global)

Ingredients:

- 2 frozen bananas
- 1 cup spinach
- 1/2 cup almond milk
- 1/4 cup yogurt (optional)
- Toppings: sliced fruits, granola, chia seeds, coconut flakes

Instructions:

In a blender, combine frozen bananas, spinach, almond milk, and yogurt. Blend until smooth and creamy. Pour the smoothie into a bowl and top with sliced fruits, granola, chia seeds, and coconut flakes. Serve immediately.

Nasi Lemak (Malaysian)

Ingredients:

- 2 cups coconut milk
- 1 cup jasmine rice
- 1/2 tsp salt
- 4 boiled eggs
- 1/2 cup sambal (chili paste)
- 1 cucumber, sliced
- Fried anchovies and peanuts for garnish

Instructions:

Rinse rice and combine it with coconut milk, salt, and 1 cup water in a rice cooker. Cook until done. Serve rice on a plate, topped with boiled eggs, sambal, cucumber slices, fried anchovies, and peanuts.

Samosas (Indian)

Ingredients:

- 2 cups all-purpose flour
- 1/4 cup vegetable oil
- 1/2 tsp salt
- Water for kneading
- Filling: 2 cups boiled potatoes, mashed
- 1/2 cup peas, cooked
- 1 tsp cumin seeds
- 1 tsp garam masala
- Oil for frying

Instructions:

In a bowl, mix flour, oil, and salt. Gradually add water to form a dough. For the filling, combine potatoes, peas, cumin seeds, and garam masala. Roll out dough and cut into circles. Place filling in the center, fold, and seal. Fry in hot oil until golden brown. Drain on paper towels and serve with chutney.

Frittata (Italian)

Ingredients:

- 6 large eggs
- 1 cup vegetables (spinach, bell peppers, etc.)
- 1/2 cup cheese (Parmesan or feta)
- Salt and pepper to taste
- 1 tbsp olive oil

Instructions:

Preheat the oven to 375°F (190°C). In a bowl, whisk eggs, salt, and pepper. In an oven-safe skillet, heat olive oil over medium heat and add vegetables. Cook until tender. Pour in the egg mixture and sprinkle with cheese. Cook on the stovetop for 2-3 minutes until the edges set, then transfer to the oven and bake until fully set, about 15 minutes. Slice and serve warm.

Huevos Rancheros (Mexican)

Ingredients:

- 4 corn tortillas
- 4 large eggs
- 1 cup salsa
- 1/2 avocado, sliced
- Fresh cilantro for garnish
- Crumbled queso fresco (optional)

Instructions:

In a skillet, lightly toast corn tortillas until warm. In another skillet, fry eggs sunny-side up. To serve, place a tortilla on a plate, top with salsa, a fried egg, avocado slices, and garnish with cilantro and queso fresco if desired.

Bircher Müesli (Swiss)

Ingredients:

- 1 cup rolled oats
- 1 cup yogurt (or milk)
- 1 apple, grated
- 1/4 cup nuts (almonds or walnuts)
- Honey or maple syrup to taste
- Fresh fruits for topping

Instructions:

In a bowl, combine rolled oats, yogurt, grated apple, nuts, and sweetener. Mix well and refrigerate for at least 30 minutes or overnight. Serve topped with fresh fruits.

French Toast (American)

Ingredients:

- 4 slices bread (thick-cut preferred)
- 2 large eggs
- 1/2 cup milk
- 1 tsp vanilla extract
- 1/2 tsp cinnamon (optional)

- Butter for cooking
- Maple syrup for serving

Instructions:

In a bowl, whisk together eggs, milk, vanilla extract, and cinnamon. Dip each slice of bread into the egg mixture, ensuring both sides are coated. In a skillet, melt butter over medium heat and cook each slice until golden brown on both sides. Serve warm with maple syrup.

Porridge (British)

Ingredients:

- 1 cup rolled oats
- 2 cups milk or water
- 1/2 tsp salt
- Toppings: honey, fruits, nuts, cinnamon

Instructions:

In a saucepan, combine oats, milk or water, and salt. Bring to a boil, then reduce heat and simmer for about 5-10 minutes, stirring occasionally until thickened. Serve warm, topped with honey, fruits, nuts, or a sprinkle of cinnamon as desired.

Dim Sum (Chinese)

Ingredients:

- 1 cup all-purpose flour
- 1/2 cup water
- 1/2 tsp salt
- Filling: 1 cup ground pork or shrimp
- 1/4 cup chopped green onions
- 1 tbsp soy sauce
- 1 tbsp sesame oil

Instructions:

In a bowl, mix flour and salt, then gradually add water until a dough forms. Knead until smooth. For the filling, combine ground meat, green onions, soy sauce, and sesame oil.

Roll out dough and cut into circles. Place a spoonful of filling in the center, fold, and seal. Steam for 15 minutes until cooked through. Serve with soy sauce or chili oil.

Arepas (Venezuelan)

Ingredients:

- 2 cups pre-cooked cornmeal (masarepa)
- 2 cups water
- 1 tsp salt
- Filling: cheese, shredded beef, or avocado

Instructions:

In a bowl, combine cornmeal, water, and salt, mixing until a dough forms. Divide into balls and flatten into discs. Cook on a hot griddle or skillet for about 5 minutes on each side until golden brown. Slice open and fill with cheese, shredded beef, or avocado.

Bagels with Cream Cheese (Jewish)

Ingredients:

- 4 cups all-purpose flour
- 2 tsp yeast
- 1 tsp sugar
- 1 tsp salt
- 1 cup warm water
- 1/4 cup baking soda (for boiling)
- Cream cheese for spreading

Instructions:

In a bowl, dissolve yeast and sugar in warm water. Add flour and salt, mixing until a dough forms. Knead for 10 minutes. Let rise for 1 hour. Shape into bagels and boil in water with baking soda for 2 minutes on each side. Bake at 375°F (190°C) for 20-25 minutes. Serve warm with cream cheese.

Misal Pav (Indian)

Ingredients:

- 1 cup mixed sprouts (moong, chana)

- 1 onion, chopped
- 2 tomatoes, chopped
- 2 green chilies, chopped
- 1 tsp ginger-garlic paste
- 1 tsp misal masala (or garam masala)
- Pav (bread rolls) for serving

Instructions:

In a pan, sauté onions until golden. Add ginger-garlic paste, green chilies, and tomatoes. Cook until tomatoes soften. Add mixed sprouts and misal masala, cooking for 10 minutes until heated through. Serve hot with pav on the side.

Gallo Pinto (Costa Rican)

Ingredients:

- 2 cups cooked black beans
- 2 cups cooked rice
- 1 onion, chopped
- 1 bell pepper, chopped
- 1 tsp cumin
- 2 tbsp salsa Lizano (optional)

Instructions:

In a skillet, sauté onions and bell peppers until soft. Add cooked beans, rice, cumin, and salsa Lizano, mixing well. Cook for 5-10 minutes until heated through. Serve as a side dish or for breakfast with eggs.

Breakfast Tacos (American)

Ingredients:

- 6 small tortillas
- 4 large eggs
- 1 cup cooked sausage or bacon
- 1/2 cup cheese (cheddar or Mexican blend)
- Salsa for serving

Instructions:

In a skillet, scramble eggs until fully cooked. Warm tortillas in another pan. Fill each tortilla with scrambled eggs, sausage or bacon, and cheese. Serve with salsa on the side.

Ramen (Japanese)

Ingredients:

- 4 cups chicken or vegetable broth
- 2 packages ramen noodles
- 1 cup sliced mushrooms
- 2 green onions, chopped
- 2 soft-boiled eggs (optional)
- Soy sauce to taste

Instructions:

In a pot, bring broth to a boil. Add mushrooms and ramen noodles, cooking according to package instructions. Serve in bowls, topped with green onions, soft-boiled eggs, and a splash of soy sauce.

Uji (Tanzanian)

Ingredients:

- 1 cup maize flour
- 4 cups water
- 1/2 cup sugar (optional)
- Milk for serving

Instructions:

In a saucepan, bring water to a boil. Gradually whisk in maize flour, stirring continuously to avoid lumps. Cook for 10-15 minutes until thickened. Sweeten with sugar if desired. Serve warm with milk.

Poff Poff (Nigerian)

Ingredients:

- 2 cups all-purpose flour
- 1/2 cup sugar

- 1 tbsp yeast
- 1/2 tsp salt
- 1 cup warm water
- Oil for frying

Instructions:

In a bowl, mix flour, sugar, yeast, and salt. Gradually add warm water to form a smooth batter. Cover and let it rise for about 1 hour. Heat oil in a deep pan and drop spoonfuls of the batter into the hot oil. Fry until golden brown. Drain on paper towels and serve warm.

Scones (British)

Ingredients:

- 2 cups all-purpose flour
- 1/4 cup sugar
- 1 tbsp baking powder
- 1/2 cup cold butter, cubed
- 1/2 cup milk
- 1/2 cup raisins or currants (optional)

Instructions:

Preheat the oven to 400°F (200°C). In a bowl, mix flour, sugar, and baking powder. Cut in cold butter until the mixture resembles breadcrumbs. Stir in milk and raisins until a dough forms. Turn onto a floured surface, roll out, and cut into circles. Bake for 15-20 minutes until golden. Serve with jam and clotted cream.

Tosti (Dutch)

Ingredients:

- 4 slices of bread
- 4 slices of cheese (e.g., Gouda)
- 4 slices of ham (optional)
- Butter for spreading

Instructions:

Spread butter on one side of each slice of bread. On the unbuttered side, layer cheese and ham if using. Top with another slice of bread, buttered side up. Heat a skillet over medium heat and grill the sandwiches until golden brown on both sides and the cheese is melted. Cut in half and serve warm.

Kanom Krok (Thai)

Ingredients:

- 1 cup rice flour
- 1 cup coconut milk
- 1/2 cup water
- 1/4 cup sugar
- Pinch of salt
- Toppings: green onions, sweet corn

Instructions:

In a bowl, mix rice flour, coconut milk, water, sugar, and salt until smooth. Heat a kanom krok pan or a non-stick skillet. Pour a spoonful of batter into each mold and cook for 2-3 minutes. Add toppings, cover, and cook until set. Serve warm.

Ceviche de Corvina (Peruvian)

Ingredients:

- 1 lb fresh corvina fish, diced
- 1/2 cup lime juice
- 1/2 red onion, thinly sliced
- 1 jalapeño, chopped (optional)
- 1/2 cup cilantro, chopped
- Salt and pepper to taste

Instructions:

In a bowl, combine diced fish, lime juice, red onion, jalapeño, cilantro, salt, and pepper. Let marinate for about 15-20 minutes until the fish is opaque. Serve chilled with corn and sweet potato on the side.

Sausage Rolls (British)

Ingredients:

- 1 lb sausage meat
- 1 sheet puff pastry
- 1 egg, beaten
- Salt and pepper to taste

Instructions:

Preheat the oven to 400°F (200°C). Roll out puff pastry and cut it into strips. Place sausage meat in the center of each strip, season with salt and pepper, and roll up tightly. Brush with beaten egg and place on a baking sheet. Bake for 20-25 minutes until golden brown. Serve warm.

Dosa (Indian)

Ingredients:

- 1 cup rice
- 1/4 cup urad dal (split black gram)
- 1/4 tsp fenugreek seeds
- Salt to taste
- Oil for cooking

Instructions:

Soak rice, urad dal, and fenugreek seeds overnight. Drain and blend into a smooth batter, adding water as needed. Let it ferment for 8 hours. Heat a non-stick skillet and pour a ladle of batter, spreading it into a thin circle. Cook until golden brown on both sides. Serve with chutney and sambar.

Tzatziki with Pita (Greek)

Ingredients:

- 1 cup Greek yogurt
- 1 cucumber, grated and drained
- 2 cloves garlic, minced
- 1 tbsp olive oil
- 1 tbsp vinegar
- Salt and pepper to taste
- Pita bread for serving

Instructions:

In a bowl, mix Greek yogurt, grated cucumber, garlic, olive oil, vinegar, salt, and pepper until well combined. Serve chilled with warm pita bread on the side for dipping.

Tamagoyaki (Japanese)

Ingredients:

- 4 large eggs
- 2 tbsp soy sauce
- 1 tbsp sugar
- 1 tsp mirin (optional)
- Oil for cooking

Instructions:

In a bowl, whisk together eggs, soy sauce, sugar, and mirin until well combined. Heat a non-stick skillet over medium heat and add a little oil. Pour a thin layer of the egg mixture into the skillet, tilting to spread evenly. Cook until the edges set, then roll it towards the edge of the pan. Add more oil and pour another layer of egg mixture, lifting the rolled egg to allow the new mixture to flow underneath. Repeat until all the egg mixture is used. Remove from the pan and slice into bite-sized pieces. Serve warm or at room temperature.

Lox and Bagel (Jewish)

Ingredients:

- 2 bagels, halved
- 4 oz lox (smoked salmon)
- 4 oz cream cheese
- 1/2 red onion, thinly sliced
- Capers for garnish
- Fresh dill (optional)

Instructions:

Toast bagel halves until golden. Spread cream cheese generously on each half. Layer with lox, red onion slices, and capers. Garnish with fresh dill if desired. Serve immediately.

Shakshuka (North African)

Ingredients:

- 2 tbsp olive oil
- 1 onion, chopped
- 1 bell pepper, chopped
- 2 cloves garlic, minced
- 1 tsp cumin
- 1 tsp paprika
- 1 can (14 oz) diced tomatoes
- 4 large eggs
- Salt and pepper to taste
- Fresh parsley for garnish

Instructions:

In a skillet, heat olive oil over medium heat. Add onions and bell peppers, sautéing until softened. Stir in garlic, cumin, and paprika. Add diced tomatoes, simmering for 10 minutes. Create small wells in the sauce and crack an egg into each well. Cover and cook until eggs are set. Season with salt and pepper, garnish with parsley, and serve with crusty bread.

Aloo Paratha (Indian)

Ingredients:

- 2 cups whole wheat flour
- 2 medium potatoes, boiled and mashed
- 1 tsp cumin seeds
- 1/2 tsp turmeric powder
- Salt to taste
- Water for kneading
- Oil or ghee for cooking

Instructions:

In a bowl, mix whole wheat flour with water to form a smooth dough. In another bowl, combine mashed potatoes, cumin seeds, turmeric, and salt. Divide the dough and filling into equal portions. Roll out a dough ball, place a portion of filling in the center, and seal it. Roll out into a flat circle. Heat a skillet and cook the paratha on both sides, applying oil or ghee until golden brown. Serve hot with yogurt or pickle.

Pão de Queijo (Brazilian)

Ingredients:

- 1 cup milk
- 1/2 cup vegetable oil
- 1 cup tapioca flour
- 2 large eggs
- 1 cup grated cheese (e.g., Parmesan or mozzarella)
- Salt to taste

Instructions:

Preheat the oven to 375°F (190°C). In a saucepan, bring milk and oil to a boil. Remove from heat and stir in tapioca flour until combined. Let cool slightly, then add eggs, cheese, and salt, mixing until smooth. Spoon the mixture into greased mini muffin tins. Bake for 15-20 minutes until puffed and golden. Serve warm.

Faworki (Polish)

Ingredients:

- 2 cups all-purpose flour
- 2 large egg yolks
- 1 tbsp sour cream
- 1 tbsp vodka (optional)
- Pinch of salt
- Powdered sugar for dusting
- Oil for frying

Instructions:

In a bowl, mix flour, egg yolks, sour cream, vodka, and salt to form a dough. Roll out thinly and cut into strips, twisting each strip into a figure-eight shape. Heat oil in a deep pan and fry the twisted dough until golden. Drain on paper towels and dust with powdered sugar. Serve as a snack.

Tteokbokki (Korean)

Ingredients:

- 1 lb rice cakes (tteok)

- 2 cups water
- 2 tbsp gochujang (Korean chili paste)
- 1 tbsp soy sauce
- 1 tbsp sugar
- 1/2 cup fish cakes, sliced (optional)
- Green onions for garnish

Instructions:

In a pan, bring water to a boil and add gochujang, soy sauce, and sugar. Stir until dissolved. Add rice cakes and cook for 10-15 minutes until softened. If using fish cakes, add them halfway through. Once the sauce thickens, garnish with green onions and serve hot.

Koshari (Egyptian)

Ingredients:

- 1 cup lentils, cooked
- 1 cup rice, cooked
- 1 cup macaroni, cooked
- 1 onion, thinly sliced
- 2 cups tomato sauce
- 1 tsp cumin
- Salt and pepper to taste
- Fried onions for garnish

Instructions:

In a skillet, heat oil and fry onions until golden brown. In a large bowl, mix lentils, rice, and macaroni. In another saucepan, heat tomato sauce with cumin, salt, and pepper. Serve the lentil mixture topped with tomato sauce and garnished with fried onions. Enjoy warm.

Poached Eggs with Spinach (Global)

Ingredients:

- 4 large eggs
- 2 cups fresh spinach
- 1 tbsp vinegar

- Salt and pepper to taste
- Olive oil for drizzling

Instructions:

Bring a pot of water to a gentle simmer and add vinegar. Crack each egg into a small bowl and gently slide them into the water. Cook for about 3-4 minutes or until the whites are set but the yolks remain runny. Meanwhile, sauté spinach in a pan with a drizzle of olive oil until wilted. Remove the poached eggs from the water and serve on a bed of spinach, seasoning with salt and pepper.

Plov (Uzbek)

Ingredients:

- 2 cups basmati rice
- 1 lb lamb, diced
- 1 large onion, chopped
- 2 carrots, julienned
- 4 cups water
- 2 tbsp vegetable oil
- 1 tsp cumin
- Salt and pepper to taste

Instructions:

In a large pot, heat oil over medium heat and add the lamb, browning on all sides. Add onions and cook until translucent. Stir in carrots, cumin, salt, and pepper, cooking for a few minutes. Add rice and water, bringing to a boil. Reduce heat, cover, and simmer for about 20 minutes until rice is tender. Fluff with a fork and serve warm.

Quiche (French)

Ingredients:

- 1 pie crust
- 4 large eggs
- 1 cup heavy cream
- 1 cup shredded cheese (e.g., Gruyère or cheddar)
- 1 cup cooked vegetables (e.g., spinach, mushrooms)
- Salt and pepper to taste

Instructions:

Preheat the oven to 375°F (190°C). In a mixing bowl, whisk together eggs and cream. Stir in cheese, vegetables, salt, and pepper. Pour the mixture into the pie crust and bake for 30-35 minutes until set and golden. Allow to cool slightly before slicing and serving.

Kachori (Indian)

Ingredients:

- 1 cup all-purpose flour
- 1/2 cup split yellow lentils, soaked and drained
- 1 tsp cumin seeds
- 1 tsp coriander powder
- 1/2 tsp garam masala
- Salt to taste
- Oil for frying

Instructions:

In a bowl, mix flour and a pinch of salt with enough water to form a smooth dough. In a blender, grind lentils with spices and salt until coarse. Divide dough into small balls, flatten, and place a spoonful of lentil filling inside. Seal and roll into a ball again. Heat oil in a pan and deep-fry kachoris until golden brown. Drain on paper towels and serve hot.

Tortilla Española (Spanish)

Ingredients:

- 4 large eggs
- 2 medium potatoes, peeled and thinly sliced
- 1 onion, thinly sliced
- Salt and pepper to taste
- Olive oil for cooking

Instructions:

Heat olive oil in a skillet over medium heat and add potatoes and onion, cooking until tender. In a bowl, whisk eggs with salt and pepper. Drain excess oil from the skillet and pour the egg mixture over the potatoes. Cook until the edges are set, then flip carefully and cook the other side until golden. Slide onto a plate and slice into wedges.

Matzah Brei (Jewish)

Ingredients:

- 4 matzos, broken into pieces
- 4 large eggs
- 1/2 cup milk (optional)
- Salt and pepper to taste
- Butter for frying

Instructions:

Soak broken matzo pieces in water for a few minutes, then drain. In a bowl, whisk eggs and milk, if using. Stir in matzo, salt, and pepper. In a skillet, melt butter over medium heat and add the matzo mixture. Cook until golden brown on both sides, flipping halfway. Serve warm, with applesauce or syrup.

Puto (Filipino)

Ingredients:

- 1 cup rice flour
- 1/2 cup sugar
- 1 cup coconut milk
- 1 tsp baking powder
- Cheese for topping (optional)

Instructions:

In a mixing bowl, combine rice flour, sugar, baking powder, and coconut milk until smooth. Pour the batter into greased muffin molds or cups, filling them halfway. Top with cheese if desired. Steam for about 15-20 minutes until set. Remove from molds and serve warm.

Breakfast Burrito (American)

Ingredients:

- 4 large tortillas
- 4 large eggs
- 1 cup cooked potatoes, diced
- 1 cup cooked sausage or bacon

- 1/2 cup shredded cheese
- Salsa for serving

Instructions:

In a skillet, scramble eggs until cooked through. Lay tortillas flat and layer with potatoes, sausage, eggs, and cheese. Roll up tightly and heat in the skillet for a few minutes until warmed through. Serve with salsa on the side.

Idli (Indian)

Ingredients:

- 1 cup idli rice
- 1/4 cup urad dal (split black gram)
- 1/2 tsp fenugreek seeds
- Salt to taste
- Water for soaking and steaming

Instructions:

Soak the idli rice, urad dal, and fenugreek seeds separately in water for about 6-8 hours. Drain and blend the urad dal with some water to a smooth batter, then add the soaked rice and blend until slightly coarse. Mix in salt and let the batter ferment overnight in a warm place. Once fermented, grease idli molds and pour the batter into them. Steam in a steamer or pressure cooker without the weight for about 10-15 minutes until cooked through. Serve hot with chutney or sambar.

Tostadas (Mexican)

Ingredients:

- 8 corn tortillas
- 1 can refried beans
- 1 cup shredded lettuce
- 1 cup diced tomatoes
- 1/2 cup grated cheese (e.g., queso fresco or cheddar)
- Salsa for topping

Instructions:

Preheat the oven to 400°F (200°C). Arrange the corn tortillas on a baking sheet and bake for about 5-7 minutes until crispy. Remove from the oven and spread a layer of refried beans on each tortilla. Top with shredded lettuce, diced tomatoes, and cheese. Return to the oven for another 5 minutes until the cheese melts. Serve topped with salsa and enjoy!